Centre for Educational Research and Innovation (CERI)

RECURRENT EDUCATION:
ITS EFFECTS ON THE AUSTRIAN EDUCATION SYSTEM

ORGANISATION FOR ECONOMIC CO-OPERATION AND DEVELOPMENT
1977

The Organisation for Economic Co-operation and Development (OECD) was set up under a Convention signed in Paris on 14th December, 1960, which provides that the OECD shall promote policies designed:
- to achieve the highest sustainable economic growth and employment and a rising standard of living in Member countries, while maintaining financial stability, and thus to contribute to the development of the world economy;
- to contribute to sound economic expansion in Member as well as non-member countries in the process of economic development;
- to contribute to the expansion of world trade on a multilateral, non-discriminatory basis in accordance with international obligations.

The Members of OECD are Australia, Austria, Belgium, Canada, Denmark, Finland, France, the Federal Republic of Germany, Greece, Iceland, Ireland, Italy, Japan, Luxembourg, the Netherlands, New Zealand, Norway, Portugal, Spain, Sweden, Switzerland, Turkey, the United Kingdom and the United States.

The Centre for Educational Research and Innovation was created in June 1968 by the Council of the Organisation for Economic Co-operation and Development for an initial period of three years, with the help of grants from the Ford Foundation and the Royal Dutch Shell Group of Companies. In May 1971, the Council decided that the Centre should continue its work for a period of five years as from 1st January, 1972. In July 1976 it extended this mandate for the following five years, 1977-82.

The main objectives of the Centre are as follows:
- *to promote and support the development of research activities in education and undertake such research activities where appropriate;*
- *to promote and support pilot experiments with a view to introducing and testing innovations in the educational system;*
- *to promote the development of co-operation between Member countries in the field of educational research and innovation.*

The Centre functions within the Organisation for Economic Co-operation and Development in accordance with the decisions of the Council of the Organisation, under the authority of the Secretary-General. It is supervised by a Governing Board composed of one national expert in its field of competence from each of the countries participating in its programme of work.

* *
*

The opinions expressed and arguments employed in this publication
are the responsibility of the authors
and do not necessarily represent those of the OECD.

© OECD, 1977
Queries concerning permissions or translation rights should be addressed to:
Director of Information, OECD
2, rue André-Pascal, 75775 PARIS CEDEX 16, France.

TABLE OF CONTENTS

Preface 5

Introduction 7

Part I

I. Summary of the paper on "Recurrent Education as an International Issue" by Gösta REHN 11

II. Summary of the paper on "Recurrent Education in the School System" by Franz PARTISCH 17

III. Summary of the paper on "Recurrent Education at Post-secondary Level" by Marian HEITGER 19

IV. Summary of the paper on "Recurrent Education from the point of view of University Management" by Sigurd HOLLINGER 23

V. Summary of the paper on "The Application of Recurrent Education to Adult Education in Austria" by Hans ALTENHUBER 25

VI. Statement by Tom SCHULLER of the OECD Secretariat . 28

Part II

I. Summary of the paper on "Recurrent Education from the point of view of Employers and Employees" by Werner SENGENBERGER 33

II. "Recurrent Education and the Employment Services": Stefan FLETZBERGER 36

III. "Recurrent Education from the standpoint of the Employer": Georg PISKATY 37

IV. "Recurrent Education from the standpoint of the Employee": Peter KOWALSKI 38

Part III

I. Report by Working Party I, H. J. Bodenhofer and
P. Kellerman: "Economic and Social Aspects of
Recurrent Education" 43

II. Report by Working Party II, A. Jedina-Palombini:
"Recurrent Education and the Employment System" 47

III. Report by Working Party III, M. Jochum and F. Partisch:
"Recurrent Education in the Education System - Structure
and Curricula" 51

Summing Up 55

List of Participants 58

PREFACE

Recurrent education has been the subject of work in the Centre for Educational Research and Innovation for several years. The first stage was conceptual, and culminated in the publication of the 'Clarifying Report' - Recurrent Education: A Strategy for Lifelong Learning (CERI/OECD, 1973). The second stage involved the preparation of the OECD report to the Ninth Meeting of the European Ministers of Education, which was held in Stockholm in June 1975 and had recurrent education as its main theme. This report was published under the title: Recurrent Education: Trends and Issues (CERI/OECD, 1975). The Ministers' endorsement of recurrent education as a basic strategy for educational planning reflected its growing acceptance in policy-making circles.

An important part of CERI's subsequent work in this field has been to promote thinking on the practical implications of that acceptance, and to this end it has been cooperating with some of the Member countries in the organisation of a number of national seminars. These seminars are designed to bring together the various parties concerned in the development of recurrent education - national or local departments of education, social affairs and labour, representatives of management and unions, teachers and researchers - to discuss the concept of recurrent education and interpret it in terms of their own country's policies and institutions.

In May 1976, one such seminar was held in cooperation with the Austrian Bundesministerium für Unterricht und Kunst, at the Bundesinstitut für Erwachsenenbildung St. Wolfgang in Strobl. This publication is an account of that seminar, and forms part of a series of reports which continue to be published on such seminars as and when they take place. It was prepared by Univ.-Prof. Dr. Marian Heitger, Prof. Werner Clement and Herbert Salaun, and has been published in Austria in: Erwachsenenbildung in Osterreich 9/76 (Bundesministerium für Unterricht und Kunst, Vienna).

INTRODUCTION

There are increasing signs that in the highly industrialized societies growth has reached a critical point, not only in the production of material goods, but also in education. The spread of schooling with the main purpose of ensuring equality of opportunity has not succeeded always and everywhere in bringing about the expected social equality. Against this background of economic and education policy limitations, national governments and international organisations have tried to develop alternatives to the present-day system of education.

An example of this is the report on "Recurrent Education" by the OECD's Centre for Educational Research and Innovation (CERI) which was on the agenda of the 9th session of the Standing Conference of European Ministers of Education (Stockholm 1975). It was an objective of that Conference to relate the concept of recurrent education to the realities of the school and education systems in the various countries.

Austria was one of the first countries to decide to hold a national Seminar on the topic of recurrent education. It was held jointly by the Federal Ministry of Education and Art and the OECD from 17th to 21st May, 1976 at the St. Wolfgang Federal Institute for Adult Education in Strobl. It would be desirable for the discussions on the reform of the Austrian school and education system to take account of the proposals made at this seminar.

Part I

I. Summary of the paper on "Recurrent Education as an International Issue" by G. Rehn (SOFI-Fack, Stockholm)

The author said that modern man felt an increasing urge towards freedom and security and he stressed that recurrent education could and should be used as an instrument for preserving human freedom and security in western industrial countries. Recurrent education was thought of as a compensation device which could improve the adaptability of the economy and the individual's freedom of movement. The "Recommendation on Active Manpower Policy" adopted by the OECD's Manpower Committee as early as 1964 had called, among other things, for more facilities for retraining and further training for gainfully employed persons of all ages, its leading idea being that an individual should be aware throughout his life that society (the State and his community, trade union and employer) would support him if he wanted to be retrained or trained up for a new kind of work.

The speaker pointed to some "strategic errors", as he called them, and unsuccessful developments, especially in the sixties, which had contributed to today's dilemma.

Problem of the "education explosion"

After economists had shown governments in the fifties that education and training were a very paying proposition for national economies (more paying than for individuals or firms) and when more and more sections of the population were increasing their demands for schooling for their children, the "education explosion" had taken place, starting in the highly industrialized countries. Almost all those countries had then made a strategic error by spending all their resources on more school education for the young. It was true that the labour market theoreticians, who under the slogan of an "active labour market policy" demanded a parallel extension of education facilities for all age groups to improve their adaptability and to be fair to all generations, had met with some understanding in some labour ministries, but budget allocations for "labour market training" were still only a small fraction of what the education ministries were able to spend on extending education for the young.

"Overloading" of secondary schools and universities

The main steps taken so far on behalf of recurrent education, namely "labour market training" and education leave, had been initiated by people outside the education system proper, but during the sixties schools and universities also had gradually moved towards a reform. The heavy flow of school children to secondary schools and of students to universities showed that those establishments were not entirely suited to the new situation. This concerned especially the Land Governments, who were prominent in committing the above mentioned strategic error.

The problem of differences in qualification levels between older and younger workers

Despite the progress mentioned above, it had to be admitted that developments in the sixties and seventies in the industrialized world had confirmed the fears of labour market theoreticians, i.e. the imbalance between the generations had worsened. At the risk of exaggerating or idealizing, one might say that the number of well-educated young persons was rising so fast that they were driving older workers out of business, but meanwhile they could not all find jobs matching their qualifications, so that they either became unemployed, or must prolong their studies contrary to plan, or must take jobs below their capacities.

Effects of the "glut of academics"

Here and there a result of making good the shortage of academics was probably to narrow wage and salary differentials, which might be welcomed as a move towards social equality, but even those who were strong supporters of "solidaristic wage policies" might consider that this result could have been achieved by less drastic methods.

The speaker went on to say that the problems under this heading must be dealt with by retraining and he described some leading aspects of a new strategy.

Preliminary considerations

An education and training system which was based on the private interests and financial resources of individuals or firms would remain below the social optimum. Fear of risk, shortage of funds and an undervaluing of higher education and training kept away the sons and daughters of too many workers from teaching facilities which could be of much value to them, while on the other hand an employer did not wish to train people who might then give some other employer the benefit of their training.

Most countries were becoming increasingly aware of those considerations and had been moving more and more towards collective arrangements for financing the costs of ever higher levels of education and training, either directly via the State budget or via special education funds (e.g. the French and British levy-grant systems). The allocation of funds for vocational training then often depended on whether the training was not just for one firm, but would also improve the mobility of the workers who received it.

The concept of educational leave

At an early stage in the history of today's trend towards recurrent education the trade unions had made a demand for paid educational leave. That demand was partly an expression of the understandable point of view that the members of the working classes, who had been under-privileged by the education system so far, and by paying taxes financed the avenues of promotion open to the so-called educated classes, should once in their lives be given the desired opportunity of getting time off for educational purposes.

As early as 1965 the trade unions had succeeded in putting the idea of paid educational leave on the agenda of the ILO, but it was not until 1974 that a convention and recommendation were adopted concerning it. Here it should be noted that the ILO records were so worded that educational leave was not formulated as an inflexible arrangement (like normal annual leave of x weeks per year which was lost if not taken in the course of the year), but rather to be taken in large slices, i.e. fairly comprehensive courses from time to time during one's working life. Thus those international pointers, while not spelling it out, meant that governments or employers could induce workers (of course by offering special benefits) to take their educational leave in periods of serious underemployment. In Sweden all workers had a legal right to training leave (and re-employment after an unspecified time). While the number of persons who could avail themselves of that right with financial support from the State was still rather limited, it was being progressively and quickly increased. Priority was given first to persons who had had little schooling in their youth.

The concept of a "second way in education" and other compensating measures

In the United States various forms of post-secondary education facilities had been developed on a large scale for balancing supply and demand in the education market. Those facilities might be described as "hybrids" between vocational and university (college) education. The speaker had specially in mind the community colleges providing mostly two-year courses, but also co-operative education consisting in alternate periods (e.g. half-yearly) periods of practice and theory. The use of television and radio had enlarged the clientele both for post-secondary and for secondary educational establishments and today a considerable proportion of students were people who had not only a school education, but also experience of a trade.

That, however, was why it was necessary to give adequate short-term retraining or further training facilities to those people who could profit from them thanks to their maturity and experience, and to encourage them to use those facilities, if it would be in their interest and would help the economy. The problem was the unforeseen changes which must be dealt with quickly, e.g. changes in skills and technical knowledge. A basic requirement was that the use of such facilities must depend on voluntary acceptance of sufficiently generous offers of new kinds of jobs.

The crux of education policy or, how can education policy and labour market policy be co-ordinated?

The speaker said he knew that many educationists declined on principle to co-ordinate labour market policy with education policy, but if that view were presented in such a way that the education system (neither general education alone nor vocational training alone) need not be regarded as the "servant of the labour market or of industry", everyone would be able to agree entirely. One must in particular avoid the "manpower approach" which assumed that it might be possible, by some forecasting technique, to tell five or ten years in advance what the economy's need for various occupational qualifications would be and that the pattern of training should then be adjusted accordingly. Reliable forecasts of this kind were not possible nor, one hoped, was a 'dirigisme' based on such an approach.

It would have been most desirable if during the sixties the leading countries had developed a stronger system for overcoming all kinds of imbalances and promoting the full utilization of all classes of manpower. Perhaps finance and economic policy-makers would not then have found it so necessary to pursue such restrictive policies for the sake of stability that there had been and would be about 5% unemployment (the average for the OECD countries) for a number of years. However, the dilemma between inflation and unemployment could not be solved as long as the funds for financing labour market policy measures were limited in most countries to a few thousandths of the GNP, and of those funds only one-twentieth or one-tenth as much was spent on quick-acting and well-designed schemes for improving the employment structure by retraining and further training adults as was spent on training youth. It was really incredible that in such major countries as Japan and Germany over 5% of the working population should be standing idle for years at a time. In order to keep the unemployed in good humour they were often paid from 70 to 90% of the purchasing power of a wage earner instead of being employed on public works or services so as to keep up their morale and fitness for work, in which case training courses would be both a cheap (and therefore non-inflationary) and a productive form of public works.

Machinery for such a policy for promoting structural balance in all sectors of the labour market could not be set up overnight. As was well known, it had taken Sweden almost 20 years, and most Swedes agreed that their capacity for ensuring full employment without inflation was not yet sufficient. Budgetary expenditure could be put at some

2% of Sweden's GNP (0.1% in the case of Austria), of which perhaps one-fifth might be regarded as spent on labour market training. It should also be stressed that the economic possibilities of developing educational establishments greatly depended on co-ordination with labour market policy and attention to labour market trends. Only by watching the continual changes in the demand for manpower could labour market authorities and educational authorities working together best help the individual, e.g. if he wanted to get out of a no longer acceptable situation by acquiring new knowledge and skills or to make better use of his abilities. On the other hand it was also clear that from the point of view of the economy and of public funds the training of adults was much cheaper and could be undertaken on a larger scale if it was given as an occupation to people otherwise unemployed, than if it involved a net withdrawal of manpower from productive work.

One further point was that as long as the number of persons of working age (15 to 65 years) who were receiving training was only 2 or 3% of the working population, it was still possible to keep education questions and labour market questions separate from one another, but that was no longer possible if the proportion was twice as great or more. Trends in the labour market such as fluctuations in total employment or changes in the pattern of employment as regards age, occupation, sex, sectors or regions, must strongly influence the flow of young persons and also older persons into the various educational establishments, as well as the inclination to remain under training. At the same time the labour market would be affected by the attractiveness of various educational establishments and the different employment opportunities they offered.

Consequently it would always seem senseless not to co-opt the education system in striving to maintain a balance in all the labour markets. The speaker was not thinking of dirigisme, but of improved vocational and student counselling and of making advantageous offers, e.g. to students in a certain category, to continue their training in cases where the capacity of the labour market to absorb people in that category did not for the present match the supply. The speaker also had in mind offers of retraining towards understaffed occupations which could otherwise become hotbeds of inflation.

If we could not cope with the task of removing any deficits and surpluses from the labour market quickly, we should be threatened with a vicious circle, because ministers of finance and economic affairs found it necessary to counter inflationary shortages with a deflationary and therefore unemployment-creating policy. The resulting unemployment acted as a strong stimulus to increasingly insistent demands for job security from those who had jobs and wished to keep them. Thus the economy became more inflexible and the gap widened between the "ins" and "outs". Changes in the structure and level of economic activity were eventually inevitable in such a "blocked society" (Chaban-Delmas had called the country he once governed "la société bloquée"). However, there was the danger that those changes would then take the form, not of gradual adjustments, but of amplified cyclical swings in production and employment and also in income distribution and prices (stagflation), which might produce more or less dramatic crises. Expensive social strife would be difficult to avoid whenever the "social contract" had to be revised so as to create a new modus vivendi.

Austrians, who had largely escaped disturbances connected with unemployment, inflation and stagnation in recent years, might perhaps find these social-philosophic reflections on the fate of western society somewhat irrelevant, but the as yet unrevealed future problems of a country could often be deduced from the experiences of other countries. Whether this applied to Austria was something which the Austrians themselves must judge. Videant consules!

In the discussion which followed there was general agreement that education policy in the sixties had led to imbalances. It therefore seemed necessary to include the social policy background when considering these problems and to point out and correct the misdirected developments and deficiencies which had arisen.

The following questions emerged during the discussion.
- What kinds of obstacles face a free-choice society?
- What form should recurrent education take in practice and how should it be put into effect?
- Should education mean acquiring documentary evidence of qualifications and entitlements leading directly to occupational results, or should it mean giving priority to the personal enrichment and self-fulfilment of the individual?
- What effective remedy is there for the difficulty of making unwilling people willing?
- How can the problem of financing be solved satisfactorily?

As the discussion centred mainly on the idea and concept of recurrent education, some basic observations were made on the task and effects of recurrent education.
- How can deficits be cured and removed by means of recurrent education?
- Are all the results of recurrent education desirable?
- Is there not a risk of confusing and equating recurrent education with lifelong learning and misdirected schooling?

Next on the programme came four short papers by experts on school education, higher education and adult education which discussed how recurrent education could be related to the establishments providing these kinds of education.

The first paper was read by Ministerialrat Dipl. Ing. Dr. F. Partisch (Federal Ministry of Education and Art, Vienna).

II. Summary of the paper on "Recurrent Education in the School System" by F. Partisch

If a discussion bearing on the topic of the Seminar was to lead to results applicable to actual situations in education, it must obviously be based on precise concepts and terms. It was therefore proposed that <u>recurrent education</u> should be taken to mean an <u>organisational system</u> whereby the working careers of the participants would be repeatedly and systematically interrupted by periods of education. (See, for example, U. Larsson, Recurrent Education, in: Permanent Education, A compendium of studies commissioned by the Council for Cultural Co-operation, Council of Europe, Strasbourg 1970. That article gave practical details and a graphic description of four possible variants of a model for recurrent education - page 415.) Consequently it was mainly adults and sometimes also more senior young people who could attend training courses organised on that recurrent principle. Of the various categories of training courses in the wide field of adult education (free education for the people, a second way in education, programmes for occupational improvement, specialization and higher qualifications) many, though doubtless not all, could clearly be organised on the recurrent principle.

As regards the connection between the <u>school system</u> and the <u>organisational principle of recurrence,</u> it would of course be irrational, uneconomic and therefore unrealistic to make it a general rule that schooling for young persons should be organised on that principle, but that did not mean that recurrent education would have no repercussions on the organisation of instruction for school children. On the other hand the pattern of recurrent education might be applied to post secondary studies such as university studies or courses in the second way in education (to allow people to take school leaving examinations in later life and obtain the corresponding entitlements). Compared with evening courses, recurrent education courses would offer clear advantages; the teaching impact would be greater and participants would not need to reside and work near where the courses were given. Comparative costs would have to be worked out, but to make it easier to organise a second way in education on the recurrent principle, arrangements would presumably have to be made when planning school curricula; for example, various school courses could be more split up, both horizontally and vertically, than hitherto in order to make the curricula better suited, as it were, for transformation into module systems.

Other relevant factors were the rapid growth of knowledge and the continual changes in the economy and society, which meant that the education processes in schools for children could in any case no longer be regarded as final. Here a recurrent education system could relieve the schools of part of their syllabus, make it unnecessary to lengthen courses or keep postponing entry into gainful employment and thereby prevent "misdirected schooling".

Lastly, recurrent education systems clearly had repercussions on school courses in that they led to increased demands on schools to promote the learner's ability to teach himself and to motivate him. Here the pupil should be made aware that what was taught about a given school subject was usually only a small fraction of the existing knowledge of it.

One certainly could not yet say in detail under what conditions and to what extent the principle of recurrent education could be applied to the school system and what repercussions it would have on it. Further detailed study would presumably be necessary before recurrent education programmes could be expressed in practical school system terms and put into effect.

The next paper was read by Professor Dr. Marian Heitger (Teacher Training Institute at Vienna University).

III. Summary of the paper on
"Recurrent Education at Post-Secondary Level"
by M. Heitger

The pruning knife must be used in order to keep within the limitations of a short paper, so that only the following four problem areas could be briefly discussed:

1. Recurrent education at post-secondary level had to be considered in connection with the prevalent education system.

2. Another question to be investigated was which general principles in recurrent education might be applicable in higher education.

3. Recurrent education at post-secondary level raised organisational and curricular problems which required close examination.

4. Finally, some critical comments would be made regarding the problem of recurrent education at post-secondary level.

Development

1. Questions of recurrent education could be considered in isolation in any part of the education system and that was especially true of so refined and sensitive a sector as higher education. Attendance at a higher education centre started at a relatively advanced age when the student had already acquired his basic experience of learning and it depended on qualifications obtained in other educational establishments. The influence of higher education centres on these qualifications and how they were acquired was only slight and indirect. Higher education centres awarded advanced degrees, etc. and their study courses often related to activities which were subject to constant change because of ongoing developments in knowledge. If recurrent education was to be an answer to that challenge, it must be able to keep pace with change, i.e. further training and advanced training must be taken into account. Thought must be given not only to the time before higher education began, but also to the time after it finished. Higher education centres could meet this requirement in two ways.

a) Their studies must be geared to the various forms of further education for purposes of recurrent education, i.e. the content and form of their studies must provide a curricular basis for further education.

b) In view of the rapid changes in vocational requirements, higher education centres must keep in closer touch than hitherto with the relevant professions in developing their facilities for advanced and further education. Various kinds of distance studies offered special possibilities, both during student years and after them as post-graduate studies.

2. Before describing the opportunities for recurrent education at post-secondary level in more detail, one should enquire into its guiding principle in that connection. Unlike the conventional education system, recurrent education believed that in a system of planned and ordered alternation it would have the following advantages, including in higher education.

2.1. When each change-over occurred, academic training could be oriented more towards the requirements of practical work than hitherto, both in the way the different study streams were planned and in the way each one of them was designed.

2.2. Education and training processes could make better use of what was learnt from specific practical experience, in respect both of motivation and of the insight and outlook derived from experience.

2.3. By continually combining theory and practice by alternating between learning and a working life the learner discovered how to apply his knowledge to what he did. Even at the study stage this combination showed how knowledge acquired and practical ability interacted; it drew no dividing line between life and school, between real situations and theorizing without responsibility.

2.4. The combination of learning and working did not keep young persons too long away from social reality and real problems in life. It might thereby prevent young people from irresponsibly building castles in the air, while protecting social reality from crystallization by preventing youthful ardour and desire for change from being sidetracked and enabling theory to be introduced with authoritative force.

2.5. The unnatural division between school and life would be removed and false intellectualization would be prevented by direct contact with practical work. The learner could discover and experience the social responsibility attaching to his knowledge and to the qualifications he had acquired or would acquire. A relationship could be re-established between policy and ability, knowledge and behaviour.

2.6. The combination of knowledge and ability with practical work could break down or mitigate the consumer-like behaviour in collecting and storing data often observed in students. They would not regard the knowledge and ability they acquired as something external, but would absorb them spontaneously in the course of their activities. Study at a higher education centre could constitute education in the sense that it imparted experience of personal and social responsibility and significance.

3. While recurrent education at post-secondary level offered advantages, its practical possibilities had still to be tested and developed.

3.1. It was a long-standing tradition in academic education that real life and studies alternated with one another in the sense that there were semesters and holidays of almost equal length, so that the organisers of that education would seem to have realized the value of its alternating rhythm. However, the rhythm was not planned for specific practical purposes and one must ask in all seriousness whether it was still adequate for today's mass universities, directly oriented as they were towards vocational qualifications.

3.2. The principle of recurrent education at post-secondary level called explicitly for the study and development of organisational arrangements for alternating between theoretical and practical training and for ways of implementing them. This applied to entrance conditions, study periods and the accompanying job-oriented practical courses. The form of education, its extent and timing would depend mainly on the speciality chosen and would have to fit in with the methods used by its practitioners, for example, doctors, engineers, lawyers, artists, teachers or even theologians and businessmen.

3.3. However, the concept of recurrent education would also influence study content and the courses would have to prepare the student for practical work and might also draw on practical experience. At all events they must always relate to real life and to the relevant sector thereof, which meant not only being directly applicable to it, but also indirectly applicable by bringing in changed attitudes and scales of values.

3.4. A close connection between real life and learning could prevent mistakes in two ways; first, by keeping the content of the syllabus in line with real requirements and secondly, by giving preference to the planning and provision of courses which took account of the needs of society.

3.5. Recurrent education could also lead to the development of short courses, if they could be divided up better. That would have two advantages; first, equality of opportunity could be improved by making courses more accessible to young persons and their parents in the lower classes and secondly, the pressure on mass universities might be reduced, so avoiding the dangers of the numerus clausus.

3.6. If theory and practice alternated regularly throughout the study period, a suitable examination system could make them better related to the qualifications demanded. Examinations would be fairer and be a better guide to future performance.

4. In conclusion, mention would be made of some difficulties, points of criticism and dangers connected with recurrent education.

4.1. A purely linear connection between theory and practice and an unconsidered limitation of the application of knowledge to man's increasing control of the world could serve only the interests of technology. They would rule out the hoped-for and expected interaction between knowledge and ability and its critical implications for <u>individual and social responsibility</u>, which would lead to less interest in humanization (Habermas: emanzipatorisches Interesse). That was why the ideal of classical education was that the student should keep away from real life and only after completing his education should he face the realities of government, technology and social affairs so as not to be corrupted by them. When one recalled that Humboldt had associated universities with that idea, one realized the importance of the problem.

4.2. A purely technical or technological or organisational combination of theory and practice would not overcome, but promote, the tendency towards a highly specialized training and produce the expert idiot. That tendency could only be countered if theory were not simply related to practice, but reflected its actual application, i.e. were assessed by the concept of interaction. Recurrent education offered opportunities for that, but so far no guarantee.

4.3. Recurrent education required curricular planning, but that planning must always be based on freedom, if it were not to lead to misdirected training in higher education centres whereby the individual's interests would be stifled and his life cast in a fixed mould.

4.4. If the curriculum were wrongly planned, the students could become uncritical, lose their creativity and fail to achieve education and autonomy. Because recurrent education was a lifelong learning process was no reason to underestimate the danger of that tendency.

A final point was that recurrent education at post-secondary level could also be an answer to the challenges of modern times. However, that answer could only be given if the academic part of the training were associated with its social responsibility. It must be understood, not as a privilege to be enjoyed, but as an achievement which carried a special responsibility and called for an education embracing training and ability, knowledge and behaviour, in which the meaning of the individual's life was seen in his responsibility towards society and in which service to the community must not be regarded as a loss of his identity.

Recurrent education could revive the classical idea that life as a whole involved tasks and that throughout one's life one could not cease asking questions and continually giving life a new meaning.

The next speaker was Dr. Sigurd Höllinger (Federal Ministry of Science and Research, Vienna).

IV. Summary of the paper on "Recurrent Education from the point of view of University Management" by S. Höllinger

University management would be interested in having a discussion of the education policy proposals accompanying the concept of recurrent education.

- 80% of the students in post-secondary education were enrolled in universities and Hochschulen (other higher education centres of university rank).

- Despite their great increase in recent years, the numbers of students and graduates in Austria were still relatively small and a further increase must be expected in the intake of universities and in the pressure on them, at least until the end of the eighties.

One could not entirely exclude difficulties in matching employment with the higher education system in the traditional categories.

Demands for a restrictive education policy might endanger the required expansion.

- The reform of conventional studies introduced by the General University Study Act was now being completed. The trends towards uniformity and formalization were being criticized and the OECD Examiners were asking for more individualization. The dialogue on the second stage of the reform had been started in the course of the OECD's country review.

It would be desirable to have a more prolonged discussion in depth of the concept of recurrent education and as many as possible of its implications. One should beware of hasty rejection or acceptance of component elements because they benefited sectional interests.

- The recurrent education programme with its objectives of "individual development and self-fulfilment, equality of opportunity, and the matching of training with practice" was a valid instrument for assessing the existing education system.

- An essential step was to make an analysis of the possible effects on society as a whole of introducing a system of recurrent education. What effects had recurrent education on the social structure?

What interests advocated it and opposed it and for what reasons? Did it involve the risk of some loss of schooling?

- It had to be seen whether and what solutions for existing problems could be provided by recurrent education, e.g. by giving education a more practical slant and reducing training costs.

- Recurrent education could not mean a programme to be planned only by experts; an important place must be given to the principles of self-organisation and co-determination.

- Recurrent education today was by no means a well-thought-out practical plan admitting of political action. It was still at the stage of a "good idea" which seemed capable of development.

The last of the four short papers was read by Ministerialrat Dr. Hans Altenhuber (Federal Ministry of Education and Art, Vienna).

V. Summary of the paper on
"The Application of Recurrent Education
to Adult Education in Austria"
by H. Altenhuber

In this paper the speaker discussed to what extent the ideas and demands of recurrent education might be of importance and value for adult education in Austria and tried to analyse individual principles and maxims of recurrent education with reference to their application and implementation within the adult education system in Austria.

1. An important principle of recurrent education was that in our dynamic society of today everybody needed lifelong learning.

Much more attention should be paid to that principle in the operation of Austria's education system. In particular, the schools should try to teach their pupils "how to learn", motivate them to seek further education and awake their interest in it. The adult education sector must be correspondingly extended, so that the right to further education did not remain a dead letter.

2. Recurrent education sought to show that, compared with school education for young persons, many of today's forms of adult education were no real alternatives as an approach to life-long learning, because only by means of a second way in education could qualifications be obtained like those awarded by schools. Consequently the whole adult education system should be planned as a broadly-based second way in education (including vocational training and further training, occupational further training and labour market training).

Such sweeping demands could not be accepted, because there would be too great a risk of misdirecting adult education as a whole and also of narrowing it down to occupational and economic requirements.

It was not the only or even the primary objective of further education to help people to acquire occupational or social entitlements and qualifications. Other important requirements had to be met, e.g. political education, cultural education, aids to developing one's personality and facing life, to name only a few.

Of the demands made, the one which would benefit and promote adult education in Austria was to improve and resolutely to extend the second way in education (organising and running it on the module system).

As an example the speaker then described a plan for extending the second way in education, in which special attention was given to modern developments and special wishes and projects connected with it.

a) Starting in the autumn of 1976, vocational training experiments would be made in schools (under the 5th school organisation regulation). These experiments would include transition courses lasting one or two semesters which could also act as courses for people in employment, and continuation courses lasting from four to six semesters with the object of passing the final examination of a vocational secondary school.

b) Pupils not obtaining a secondary school qualification would also be given the opportunity of matriculating after completing a special ten-month preparatory course.

c) Other projects were:
- to design a second way in education for adults
- to create additional second way facilities (with a wide geographical spread), especially in the vocational training sector
- to develop corresponding educational programmes in the media (ORF-Akademie)
- to put legal controls on distance studies
- to make more use of the module system in education through co-operation between schools and adult education
- to extend educational information and counselling services for adults
- to give better financial support to participants in the second way in education
- to extend the system of final examinations for external students (e.g. at technical and commercial colleges) and examinations for vocational qualifications (e.g. at primary teacher training colleges).

3. Recurrent education required that lifelong learning after compulsory schooling, i.e. all adult education, should be organised as a periodic alternation between training and practice.

Here much depended on releasing workers for educational activities; whether they were released and with what success would largely decide whether this requirement of recurrent education would be more widely met. Even in future, however, a considerable part of further education would doubtless take the form, not of a "periodic alternation between training and practice" with release from work, but of leisure-time education, i.e. after working hours.

4. Recurrent education would like to build a comprehensive structural, organisational and planning framework for the hitherto rather unrelated parallel systems of vocational training and further training in schools (including labour market training) and general adult education.

Such a comprehensive education plan would certainly be desirable for Austria. As regards adult education, it should be remembered that the sponsoring organisations and facilities were autonomous, but it was nevertheless possible as well as necessary to increase the co-operation between those facilities and between school and adult education, both in planning and in practice. In Austria the foundations for that already existed, for example:

- the Konferenz der Erwachsenenbildung Österreichs (KEBÖ)
- the "AHS für Berufstätige" project group in the BMUK
- planning and implementation of media programmes (the future ORF-Akademie)
- co-operation between school libraries and public libraries, etc.

VI. Statement by the OECD Secretariat

Following these four short papers, Tom Schuller (OECD, Paris) made a statement. He stressed that recurrent education required long-term development planned in advance, in which the education sector and the world of employment should be regarded, not as separate sectors, but as necessarily and closely interconnected with one another.

The two could best be fused by the following measures.

- General access to recurrent education should be guaranteed especially by supporting measures including the recognition of working experience and experience of life..
- The teaching method contemplated for recurrent education must be suited to the specific requirements of adults.
- That meant introducing and creating more problem-oriented study courses.
- More must be done to establish and organise recurrent education on the module principle.
- Here much depended on attracting a suitable body of teachers, who must be helped in their endeavours to continue their own training.
- The right to educational leave must not be tied only to occupational further training, but must also be granted for purposes of general education.
- Lastly, there should be increased co-operation between ministries, employers' federations and trade unions leading to a better and more rational use of existing facilities.

After these five papers, which raised and discussed many problems and questions, the speakers confined themselves mainly to matters of principle and attempts to define recurrent education. A pressing need was felt for wording to clarify the concept of "recurrente Bildung". During the discussion three separate questions and topics emerged:

- To which groups of objectives should priority be given?
- Which statements of objectives should be regarded as authoritative?
- On what time intervals should recurrent education be based?

Competition between adult education and recurrent education could be avoided and neutralized at the start by clearly separating their functions. Nor must recurrent education be understood and developed as an extension of the system for obtaining qualifications and entitlements. Some rethinking was required so that recurrent education might be regarded as an <u>alternative possibility</u>.

The Seminar continued with a paper by Professor Dr. Werner Sengenberger (Institute for Social Science Research, Munich).

Part II

I. Summary of the paper on "Recurrent Education from the point of view of Employers and Employees" by W. Sengenberger

Introductory remarks

As there was a close and interdependent connection between the education system and the employment system, those two systems should not be treated independently of one another. Likewise, education policy and labour market policy should be merged.

For various reasons, especially analytical, the speaker would deal mainly with occupational education for adults, altough it could. not easily be separated from general and political education, which might be a prerequisite or basis for vocational education.

Three main theses:

1. Employers and employees associated a number of their own interests with further education and pursued them through it.

2. The interests of the two groups in further education were to some extent opposed and a subject of dispute. The main disagreement today was not whether there should be further education, but on how it should be provided. The issue was not the objective, but how further education should be utilized and designed.

3. Disagreement today concerned mainly how much further education should be provided, the conditions for access to it, its content, and how costs and returns should be distributed.

Here what was meant was not primary school and vocational education and informal instruction given on the job within the production process, but all formal post-basic education given outside the production process.

The employer's interest in further education

It was a means of ensuring that sufficient manpower of adequate quality was available at all times. Employers had become interested in further education because of
- the need for different qualifications owing to structural changes in technology and industry

- a manpower shortage in inter-enterprise sectoral labour markets
- employees' expectations regarding promotion, more job security and a higher income
- increasing legal controls on primary vocational training and limitation of the entrepreneur's freedom of action.

Enterprises tried, by influencing the design and organisation of further education (in the Federal Republic of Germany they did most to operate and finance it),
- to raise qualifications as much as possible
- at minimum cost
- with a minimum risk that the trainees would leave their employment
- whilst limiting the demand for better pay.

This they did by influencing the selection of participants or target groups, by binding participants by contract, by pay policies, by controlling study content and by awarding no certificates for taking further education courses.

The employee's interest in further education

1. It maintained and improved his productivity and made him more adaptable and mobile.

2. Social equality meant evening out unequal job opportunities due to unequal access for employees to primary education.

3. It brought political and social emancipation and equipped the employee better for protecting his own and his group's interests.

These employee's interests had been little served by further education in its existing form and it must be recast to achieve the desired objectives.

So far, further education:
- had not met the requirement for counter-cyclical assistance (in bridging over periods of unemployment);
- had tended more to widen than close the gap between levels of qualification and pay by assisting mainly employees who were already well-qualified and neglecting those with low qualifications;
- had tended to impart too narrow qualifications geared to the enterprise's own purposes instead of broad basic qualifications;
- had led to an unfair distribution of costs and returns at the expense of employees and the State or its employment services.

In those respects further education (and all kinds of recurrent education) must be changed so as to be able to serve the employee's interests.

Following Dr. Sengenberger's paper came three short statements by:

- Ministerialrat Dr. Stefan Fletzberger
  (Federal Ministry of Social Affairs, Vienna)

- Dr. Georg Piskaty
  (Science and Education Policy Department of the Federal Chamber of Commerce, Vienna)

- Dr. Peter Kowalski
  (Labour Market Training Institute, Vienna).

The following are extracts from these statements.

II. "Recurrent Education and the Employment Services":
S. Fletzberger

A statement of the employment services would hardly be expected to make a direct contribution to the discussion of the effects of recurrent education on the education system. This statement, apart from making some general points, would therefore describe such activities of the employment services as might be regarded as connected with recurrent education.

The Labour Market Improvement Act laid down the objectives of "income security", "free choice of job (and occupation)", "a well-considered choice of job (and occupation)" and "productive employment", in accordance with which the employment services naturally tried to offer everyone in the labour market a suitable job or occupation and to offer employers a choice of candidates. Each year the order of priority for the measures to be taken was revised. For example, top priority in 1976 went to measures for

helping to prevent unemployment
smoothing the path of newcomers to the labour market
helping special categories of manpower, especially handicapped persons. *

One of the most effective instruments for giving effect to these measures was vocational education and the following activities might be mentioned in connection with the subject of the statement.

1. Planning and promotion of study courses and distance study courses, etc., and having them run by schooling facilities as a measure for preventing lay-offs and short-time working (education to absorb manpower).

2. Promotion of in-plant education as a precaution against longer-term employment difficulties.

3. Planning and providing, or assisting and appointing others to provide, vocational further training by means of post-school instruction and studies and courses for acquiring the full qualifications for a teaching occupation (short courses for skilled workers) in order to meet the current needs of industry and as so-called preventive education.

---

* Depending on economic developments, high priority would again be given in 1977 to measures for improving manpower qualifications through further education.

III. "Recurrent Education
from the standpoint of the Employer":
G. Piskaty

On the basis of the OECD's rather vague idea of recurrent education and the rather wide concepts described in the Seminar, it was not easy for employers to adopt a definite attitude and they had not done so officially. The following remarks would therefore try to set out the pros and cons of implementing the idea, having regard to the main features of the OECD's concept and of the Austrian employers' basic position on education policy.

Two points should first be made. On the one hand almost everyone, whether formally or informally, continued his own education, and that process might be underestimated in planning recurrent education. On the other hand one should remember that Austria had already made various moves towards recurrent education (see below), including the education provided by industry as part of vocational education for adults (WIFI, etc.) and also by enterprises.

What <u>advantages</u> might industry derive from giving effect to some of the main features of recurrent education?

- Recurrent education might give better opportunities to everyone who had interrupted his education and wanted to re-enter the education system after periods of employment. Here recurrent education might lead to more liberal conditions of access to the education system, such as industry had for long been demanding. More distant study facilities should be created and there should be more special arrangements for making higher education accessible to persons who had proved their worth in working life.

- Recurrent education required better co-operation between the education system and the employment system, and hence more attention to the requirements of industry in planning curricula.

- The repeated demands for lengthening the first way in education (a 13th school year and a 6-semester training course for primary school teachers) would lose their force.

- For certain categories whose previous training had not brought them into touch with industrial practice, e.g. teachers, compulsory practical courses could make good their lack of contact with industry.

IV. "Recurrent Education from the Standpoint of the Employee": Peter Kowalski

The interests of Austrian wage and salary earners must be protected. Although the policy for full employment held the stage, other trade union demands must not be neglected or downgraded. Trade union policy should be equated with overall policy, hence recurrent education could not be treated in isolation from other parts of the education system. Attention should first be given to study content, which in practice meant pressing on with school reform for 10 to 18 year-olds. Recurrent education should be regarded as part of a broad policy and conflict must be avoided between employees who had received recurrent education and others who had not. Trade unions could not agree to a system which resulted in inequality of status and insecurity.

The unsolved questions and problems of entitlement must be settled in the near future. The systematic result of recurrent education should be to achieve the goal of autonomy for the employee.

After these short statements the participants joined in the discussion and agreed that the labour market and the school system should no longer be regarded and discussed as separate systems. Purely structural alterations to the present system would certainly not have the desired success. First attention must be given to investigating and working out study content.

In this connection suggestions were made regarding the curriculum and organisation of types of school for 10 to 14 year-olds which could be connected with pioneering models of preparatory vocational education. Finally, it was suggested that it would be better not to seek rigid definitions of recurrent education, but to develop strategies pragmatically.

The participants in the Seminar then formed themselves into three working parties which dealt with the following subject areas:

Working Party I

"Economic and social aspects of recurrent education" chaired by Professor Dr. H.J. Bodenhöfer.

Working Party II

"Recurrent education and the employment system" chaired by Frau Professor Dr. Auguste Jedina-Palombini.

Working Party III*

"Recurrent education in the education system - structure and curricula" chaired by Ministerialrat Dipl.-Ing. Dr. Franz Partisch and Dr. Manfred Jochum.

The following day and a half were allocated to the working parties' studies.

---

* Originally a fourth working party was planned to cover the subject area "Recurrent education - curricula, methods and media" (chaired by Dr. M. Jochum), but because of the number of participants it was merged with Working Party III.

Part III

I. Report by Working Party I:
H.J. Bodenhöfer - P. Kellermann
"Economic and Social Aspects of Recurrent Education"

1. As regards its concept, recurrent education was taken to mean a plan for general reforms which sought to put into practice the principles of lifelong learning - by means of a guaranteed recurrence of periods of organised learning distributed over the lifespan of the individual - and to dovetail learning in school with learning out of school. Its second feature was that it meant utilizing educational opportunities in all spheres of community life and relating school learning to practical work, with curricular consequences for the entire school system.

The Working Party would not agree to narrow the scheme down to the principle of distributing consecutive educational courses of fixed duration after compulsory school age between separate periods of education sandwiched with practical work. In practical terms, recurrent education could assume a variety of forms, some of which had already emerged within the existing system, while others were demanded as alternative reforms (e.g. a system of organised vocational further education, an extension of the second way in education, educational leave of absence, extended adult education, etc.). The distinctive feature here was that workers, especially adults, should be enabled to re-enter the education system - repeatedly - by means of bridges and transitions aided by suitable financial and organisational measures.
At the same time it should be arranged that young persons would be offered a real alternative between starting employment and spending more time in the education system.

2. The discussion of the economic and social aspects of recurrent education turned on a number of major problem areas and questions.
   - What economic arguments are relevant to the concept of recurrent education and what are the economic aspects of its objectives?
   - Are criteria for assessing a system of recurrent education obtainable from cost-benefit analysis?
   - What financing problems and what alternative financing models have to be investigated in order to introduce systems of recurrent education?
   - What results and consequences are to be expected from a system of recurrent education,

for the individual (alienation, participation and self-fulfilment, broken down by sex, age, religion, occupation,, etc.),

for institutions (entreprises, group interest representation, and organisation of the policy-making process, especially in education),

for the community as a whole (social structure, the school system, industry, the employment system, the labour market, culture, administration, etc.)?
- Which of them must be studied in detail in order to decide what reform measures to take?

Here economic and social policy perspectives provided complementary material for evaluating a system of recurrent education and their positive and negative effects must be weighed up with reference to overriding objectives.

Among the economic arguments for recurrent education and the economic objectives it pursued were the obsolescence and updating of vocational knowledge and skills, as well as the opportunities it gave for making informed decisions repeatedly and step by step regarding education processes.

A system of recurrent education seemed specially well suited for dealing with unemployment caused by economic recessions. It was a function of the education system to avoid the consequences of unemployment (demoralization of the unemployed, social conflict, etc.).

It was likewise a function of the education system to solve unemployment problems which were caused by structural and technological factors and arose during the structural change accompanying economic growth (adaptation of qualifications, retraining, etc.). Recurrent education had special responsibilities and facilities for finding jobs for certain categories (such as immigrant workers, or reinstating women, and employed and self-employed persons in rapidly declining sectors - small businessmen, farmers, etc). and generally for using education processes as an instrument for social integration and for giving special assistance to the under-privileged and handicapped.

3. The fact that there was general interdependence between the education system and the employment system meant that a study must be made of the effects of recurrent education on the employment system. The main value of transfers from the education system to the employment system lay in making jobs more accessible by reducing the division of labour (job enlargement and job enrichment), by changing job organisation and communications structures and by changing the content of some jobs. In other words, a greater contribution to "humanizing working life" might be expected from a system of recurrent education than from more traditional systems of organising education processes.

In connection with the relationship between the education system and the employment system, recurrent education must also be seen as a strategy for solving the problem of people who were wholly or partially over or under-qualified for potential jobs. As against the thesis that there was a glut of academics, a shortage of skilled workers, etc., there was the thesis that in many sectors those employed were under-qualified, which assumed that in many cases the level, breadth and direction of training did not satisfy the real requirements of jobs today or of what might be demanded of them. Of special importance were changes in income (pay) structure (levelling or differentiating?) and the development of technical innovation, which depended on the availability and qualifications of the personnel.

4. In evaluating the financing problems and alternative financing models for a system of recurrent education one must start by considering expected resource requirements, the possible ways of sharing the burden, and the effects of different financing methods.

As regards the growing expenditure on education, the transition to a system of recurrent education would mean higher overall figures, especially for subsistence allowances (or compensation for loss of income) in the latter stages of study. Consequently, the entire education system would have to be subsidized in order to keep down costs. There were several sources or methods of financing total educational expenditure:
- the State: by general tax revenue, special or purpose-linked taxes, and loans;
- enterprises: by self-financing of educational activities including indirect costs (continued wage payments), payment of special dues to the State, and financing by a fund fed by contributions;
- private households: by partial acceptance of the costs (fees, etc.) and lost income, and repayable loans.

A study should be made of the economic, social and political effects of these schemes. Of special importance were the implications for the organisation (planning, execution and monitoring) and direction of education processes (content), as well as for the income distribution effects of the method of financing (regressive or progressive effects on personal income distribution). A necessary first step would be to analyse the current arrangements for financing education, which were largely unknown (total education expenditure, burden-sharing, income distribution effects, etc.).

One of the factors determining how the costs of a system of recurrent education should be distributed between the State, enterprises and private households would be the objectives and practical uses of individual courses and study periods. Here the following two points were still controversial. First, in view of the increasing importance of skilled manpower in production, enterprises should be asked to finance a larger share of the costs. Secondly, the financing of education should be regarded as ultimately a part of the government's overall redistribution policy and an education policy which pursued the social policy aim of real equality of opportunity in life made it desirable to charge more of the cost to private persons.

5. From the social policy angle, the concept of recurrent education should be considered with reference to its ability to secure loyalty to and identification with the existing social, political and economic systems. From that overall community point of view it should be asked whether the ability of a recurrent education system to secure loyalty should be rated higher than that of traditionally organised education processes and whether the social system was in increasing need of justification which recurrent education should help to provide.

6. The Working Party proposed to institute a body to act as an advisory and co-ordinating centre for initiating, discussing and recommending proposals, measures of reform and corresponding investigations. One of its main study areas would be the interdependence between the education and employment systems and co-ordination between education and employment policies, having due regard to their social policy aspects.

The next statement was by Paul Kellermann and concluded the Working Party's report, but time did not allow it to be discussed and correspondingly amended for the record. The following paragraph reproduces what he said.

As regards the social policy aspects of recurrent education, discussion and attention should concentrate on how to centralize control of the acquisition of qualifications and the processes of production and integration by means of an expanded system of recurrent education. One should not overlook the value of a network of training courses, a ladder of certificates, diplomas, etc. and periodic spells of further education on the module principle interwoven with the employment system as an instrument for wielding centralized control. A study should be made of their possible effects in determining access to further education (e.g. as an alternative to the numerus clausus), in aggravating or reducing social tensions and in building up or maintaining loyalty towards the traditional social system. It was just when recurrent education was to serve to mitigate or partially abolish the negative effects of nationalization carried so far forward mainly by economic interests, that it was important to examine carefully whether such education, with all its implications for all members of society, was compatible with the goals of a social and humane democracy and whether its compatibility could be guaranteed by institutional means. Here one must beware of over-hastily adopting for purely pragmatic reasons some elements in a system which were destined to serve a comprehensive scheme for recurrent education, and also of quasi-automatic trends towards such a system which were not subject to public discussion.

II. Report by Working Party II:
A. Jedina-Palombini
"Recurrent Education and the Employment System"

1. Recurrent education - a definition

The starting point for the discussion was the OECD's definition of recurrent education as alternating periods of education and practice. Thematically, the training should be regarded in the long term as more than vocational education and as including general education and civic education, as well as traditional adult education. In view of the periods of instruction it would involve during working life, there should not normally be a need to lengthen school education. The discussion was confined to questions connected with working life.

2. Recurrent education in the employment system

The alternation between education and practice must not lead to a detrimental splitting up of an education planned as a whole. Three timing variants were envisaged:

a) employment before further education
b) employment during further education
c) practical instruction as part of further education.

By employment was meant all kinds of work for ensuring survival, so that it normally included both independent members of a family and members helping at home, as well as housewives, all of whom should be given the same facilities. The organisation of recurrent education should be built up on existing facilities, especially those for adult education, and on plans made by the employment services and school administration authorities. Cognizance should also be taken of infirm and inter-enterprise educational facilities, whose scope and teaching content should be enriched and extended, having due regard to the common interests of employers and employees.

Co-operation between the different schemes should be ensured by consultation in a single forum. The question was discussed whether and at what stage legislation additional to the Labour Market Improvement Act and the Adult Education Act might be required.

Much attention was given in the discussion to the question of motivation. A condition for motivation was a sound general education and that called for general improvement in people's ability and readiness to assimilate education.

Motivation should also be improved by stressing the conceptual aspects of work (participation in job design, self-organisation, self-controlled work performance, rotation procedures, group education, etc.). The world of work must be humanized, if lack of motivation were to be remedied, and here it should be remembered that strong incentives to further education could come from interest in one's career (promotion or a better mastery of one's job).

The employment services' experience with schooling schemes for absorbing manpower showed that instruction given to improve motivation could be successful, and suitable training courses could lead to employment.

Such education could be based on retraining called for by the changing structure of industry and on (in-firm and external) later instruction, e.g. for women resuming a working life. Women should be regarded as a specially important target group, whose switching from employment to marriage and a family and later back to employment required repeated spells of instruction. Other special target groups were both young and older employed persons, who might have problems, as experience had shown. A major function of recurrent education was to prevent people from losing ground in their occupations, as there was a risk in the most widely differing sectors of becoming less qualified.

The discussion showed that a risk was seen that education might become more polarized through its connection with recurrent education. That risk should be countered by suitable measures to increase motivation.

As regards study content, it appeared desirable to combine vocational education with basic elements in practical aids to living in order to enable people to cope with their private, occupational and social problems. That should appeal to the individual as a whole and help him to develop all his abilities. The question was discussed whether any commitment to do that should be envisaged and arguments for and against were advanced, including the drawbacks of having a medley of themes in a completely target-oriented education.

3. Recurrent education with reference to the education and employment systems

A number of factors could be found in Austria which favoured a system of alternating between education and practice, including the dual system used (partly) in training apprentices, a composite system of courses for school training, e.g. in agriculture and forestry, practical study periods in secondary vocational schools and vocation-related courses for secondary school leavers, as well as many services provided by adult education facilities, distance study schools and courses through the media.

It was true that recurrent education must normally have repercussions on the content, methods and organisation of the education system. The demands on the latter included:
- better co-ordination of the education system with the quantitative and qualitative requirements of the employment system;
- laying the foundations for the required ability and readiness to assimilate education;
- relevant information on education and occupations, together with appropriate counselling.

4. Effects of recurrent education

Recurrent education had widely differing effects which would have to be worked out more thoroughly and tested. The following problem areas were discussed:
a) personal problems,
b) problems in the enterprise,
c) problems for the national economy.

a) Personal problems:

- questions of labour law (pay claims, leave claims, claims for compensation payments on termination of contract, safeguarding jobs or keeping them free, counting study as working hours)
- questions of social insurance law (sickness insurance, accident insurance, pension insurance, unemployment insurance, extended insurance, contribution and substitution periods)
- occupational and social opportunities
- development of personality.

b) Problems in the enterprise:

- organisational changes (outflow of semi-skilled workers and manpower substitution)
- increased in-plant training
- inclusion of all personnel in recurrent education schemes
- safeguarding jobs and keeping them free
- problems involved in reinstating employees
- cost and financing problems.

c) Problems for the national economy:

In considering the national economy aspects it should be remembered that the dominant structure in Austria was one of small and medium-sized enterprises. That meant that the inclusion of self-employed persons in recurrent education would affect the economy as a whole and would therefore affect the solution of the problems for enterprises.

National economy criteria included the following:
- safeguarding full employment
- preventing unemployment

- preserving the ability of enterprises to compete internationally
- reduction in labour productivity
- qualitative improvement in production
- (ideally) an increase in the GNP by raising the level of general education.

The employers' federations and trade unions would have to make important contributions to solving these problems (under a), b) and c)).

The employment services could try to solve many of the above problems by providing trainees for a trade in exchange for applicants for recurrent education.

5. Recurrent education and educational leave of absence

The discussion had shown that it was essential for an examination of recurrent education problems to include the question of educational leave of absence. Both those subjects must therefore be discussed jointly, because they were directly interconnected and to some extent overlapped.

A number of effects connected with educational leave of absence had already been discussed and could be fed into the model for finding a solution. Educational leave of absence might become a valuable step towards making recurrent education a reality, which could only be done through a dynamic process of development which would call for many more studies.

III. Report by Working Party III:
M. Jochum - F. Partisch
"Recurrent Education in the Education System
Structure and Curricula"

The Working Party agreed to take the OECD paper* as a starting point and discuss how far the idea of recurrent education in that paper might affect Austria's overall system, especially secondary education, non-university and university post-secondary education and adult education.

The first step was to discuss the paper's suggestions regarding:
- development and autonomy for the individual
- more equality of opportunity
- better liaison between education and the world of work, and
- periodic alternation between employment and education as part of a new organisation for learning

as well as the implicit objectives of making political and social life less rigidly hierarchical as regards:
- status
- income, and
- occupation

by means of recurrent education. However, the Working Party considered that its first task was not to interpret the OECD paper, but to discuss it in connection with new trends in education in Austria.

1. Secondary education

The Working Party could not identify itself with the demand in the OECD paper (page 28, e) that "it should be possible and important to pursue any career in an intermittent way, meaning an alternation between study and work".

The Working Party was of the opinion that, apart from the apprenticeship training already given intermittently under the dual system and apart from various organisational patterns for the second way in education, one should reject "interruption" as a "guiding principle", even in cases where it was regarded as an essential factor in recurrent

---

* Recurrent Education - A Strategy for Lifelong Learning, OECD, Paris, 1973, translated into German under the title "Ausbildung und Praxis im periodischen Wechsel (Recurrent Education) and issued by the Secretariat of the Standing Conference of Land Education Ministers in the Federal Republic of Germany.

education and a self-evident one in the education process. It was noted that by dropping certain final examinations in secondary education one would be unlikely to promote rational recruitment for practical work and thereby challenge a leading idea in recurrent education (i.e. the idea of building up a succession of education cycles sandwiched with spells of employment, as in the module system). However, the Working Party considered that the present timing for leaving the education system successfully should be shortened for purposes of recurrent education, so far as was compatible with the educational value of the school concerned.

It was pointed out that the upper forms of secondary schools offered a range of possibilities for recurrent education, especially under the Fifth Amendment to the School Organisation Act.

Summary

1.1. The Working Party considered that for purposes of recurrent education
- it should be made possible to interrupt schooling at secondary level and easy to return to it;
- this procedure should be neither condemned nor held up as a desirable goal;
- as far as possible the conclusion of certain periods of education should be timed so that the subsequent spells of practical work could be built into later education cycles leading to a qualification.

1.2. The Working Party recommended that the education authorities should discuss principles a-d and f-h on page 28 of the OECD paper, mainly in order to see how many of them had already started to be adopted by the Austrian education system and which of them could be implemented by making relatively slight changes to the existing system.

1.3. The Working Party accepted the idea of alternation between education and practice and saw important services it could render in providing motivation for education and altering the mentality of the Austrian population, but did not agree that it was desirable for people to leave and re-enter the education system at secondary school level as and when they wished.

2. Post-secondary education

a) Transition to university education

Recurrent education would have to make access to university studies easier for all those who had not matriculated. The present situation as regards the matriculation examination was in any case unsatisfactory, but even the proposal now under discussion for an examination conferring the right to study was inadequate for purposes of recurrent education. The proposed limitation to a particular percentage of applicants should be dropped and in the interests of social and regional equality of opportunity the validity of preparatory courses should not be restricted to a few of the more important places in Austria.

It was also pointed out that the period of practical work between secondary and post-secondary education, as desired for recurrent education, was perfectly possible in Austria and was indeed being put into effect.

b) Transition to non-university post-secondary education

Here much the same applied as to the transition to university education. The Working Party recommended that access should be granted (as required for recurrent education) to those without school leaving certificates, as was already done in individual cases (e.g. the preparatory course for entering the Academy of Social Studies).

c) University education

Not least in connection with the current problems of drop-outs, the idea should be discussed of restructuring university courses on the lines of module systems, leading perhaps to conclusions regarding credits for qualifications obtained at secondary level or non-university post-secondary level or in practical work.

It should also be considered whether higher education centres should not be broadened so as to provide education for persons without formal entrance qualifications. Steps in that direction had already been taken in providing university education for adults and vocation-oriented special courses (higher education courses), but much more should be done.

The vocation-oriented study facilities following a first degree should be further extended and might be made an alternative to studying for a doctor's degree.

As regards the training and further training of university teachers, there were features favouring the principle of recurrence both in non-university and in university post-secondary education whose further development should be considered. Not the least important question to discuss was how far temporary activities outside teaching activity were desirable and useful as a means of getting into closer touch with practical work.

The Working Party also noted that an important function of the universities was to give further education to graduates on the recurrent principle and considered that they should do this on a larger scale than hitherto. By so doing they might be expected to be able to obtain fruitful guidance from people exercising a profession or trade.

3. Adult education

In the whole system of recurrent education which should embrace school education including dual-system training, non-university post-secondary education and especially adult education, the latter was of fundamental importance. In certain particular ways, adult education had provided experience which could serve as a guide in planning a system of recurrent education. Its programmes were varied and flexible, it was usually geared to the needs and expectations of adults, and access to it was usually in line with the special personal, economic and social situations and circumstances of its clientele.

However, the Working Party did not consider that all the purposes of adult education would be fulfilled by the proposal in the OECD paper that adult education as a whole should be regarded merely as a part of a comprehensive system of vocational and further education and should be governed mainly by labour market requirements.

In planning adult education more attention should be given to those aspects which affected equality of opportunity for those categories who were handicapped under the present education system. The authorities responsible for adult education should be asked to build on existing models and develop new ones. Examples of questions requiring attention were the improvement of the second way in education and a decision to extend it, education programmes through the media and certification on the lines of a module system. A further task of adult education would be to react quickly and sensitively to the requirements and demands of social life and to include technology and O and M in its programmes for recurrent education.

4. Conclusions

Owing to shortage of time and the complexity of the problems in adult education this topic could not be treated fully during the Seminar and the Working Party recommended that it should be further discussed by institutions for adult education.

For the purposes of a comprehensive system of recurrent education isolated measures taken in the education sector were mostly not on target. In all these questions it was of key importance to introduce educational leave of absence, and for new developments to occur, still higher importance must be attached to motivation and counselling or education information. However, the Working Party considered that all these problems could only be handled and solved by planning a comprehensive system of recurrent education and with co-operation between all the parties concerned or affected.

After the Working Parties had made their reports, there followed a discussion of the main points in them.

SUMMING UP

Concluding the Seminar, Professor Dr. Heitger summed up in a short closing speech the stage reached in the discussion, its starting points and results.

He stressed five points.

1. The question of motivation for recurrent education

Recurrent education should be regarded as an attempt to give an educator's answer to the challenge of the knowledge explosion. It must initiate expert learning to enable people to achieve autonomy.

It should be remembered that the question of social justice in a community seemed closely interconnected with the problem of equality of opportunity in the education system, which meant that the present gap between the education and employment systems must be bridged. An example of this unsolved discrepancy could be seen in the burning issue of drop-outs.

The continuing and increasing alienation of human beings in today's life process called for some quick thinking which recurrent education could not escape, if it were not to become the plaything of social forces and eventually join in the alienation process itself.

2. Recurrent education's attempts at answering this challenge

Recurrent education aimed at a periodic alternation between learning and real life situations whereby an individual's accumulated experience could be used in the process of educating him. That meant also that explicit efforts must be made to bridge the gap between school and life often found under the present school system. People must learn by experience that they can and must take what they learn into practical life and vice versa. The acquisition of knowledge and ability could not be considered independently and separately from social responsibility, but most be expressly related to it in several respects:

- as motivation, by explaining to people the theoretical basis of their practical real-life situations;
- as a matter of content, by trying to analyse the substance of the problems which actuate human beings and thereby find a causal basis for what is experienced, which could be used again for further developments;
- successful learning also meant not ruling out personal questions, but deliberately looking for them and asking them.

3. Organisational and structural questions concerning recurrent education

The danger that human beings might become prisoners of their own technology must be countered by humanely designing and organising the situations and conditions in which production took place. Co-operation between employers and employees, which at present was governed largely by economic considerations, should include the wider social factors which moulded an education system.

If people in employment were to be given sound educational advice which endeavoured to take account of their individual needs, possibilities and inclinations, the first step was to develop and provide a wide range of educational facilities.

- The idea of recurrent education should be included in basic education (e.g. learning to learn, which might have favourable effects on preserving the motivation to learn).
- Matriculation should be planned more in association with work and life experience.

Here recurrent education could be understood and provided in three ways:

- recurrent education related to one's occupation
- recurrent education as an adjunct to one's occupation
- recurrent education as an alternation between periods of learning and work.

4. Methods and instruments of recurrent education

It was generally assumed that before deciding for or against practical methods and instruments, agreement must be reached on a classification system for the content of training and education.

That was not necessary, because normally all study content was suitable for education, but the assumption led to further consequences for a) methodology and pedagogics on the one hand, and b) teacher-pupil relations on the other hand.

As regards a), methodology and pedagogics should show that by learning a given syllabus one could learn the art of learning itself, i.e. methodically disciplined reasoning on the subject. That should not be regarded as a technique, but as valid reasoning on a given subject in a given area (concept of transfer).

As regards b), formal learning included a process of reciprocal reasoning. Someone who had learnt how to reason had also learnt how to learn more.

5. Future and possible effects of recurrent education

Recurrent education was a definite idea of education and further education for people in connection with their real-life situations and it would be most dangerous to give it a purely technological meaning in the sense of the acquisition and application of knowledge.

An organisation should be set up to discuss all the questions which had been raised about recurrent education and incorporate the positive features of the Austrian education system in this new development.

LIST OF PARTICIPANTS

Altenhuber, Min.-Rat. Dr. Hans,
   Head of the Adult Education Department in the Federal Ministry of Education and Art, Wallnerstrasse 8, 1010 Vienna.

Blaschek, Dr. Hannelore,
   Institute for Adult Education, Imbergstrasse 24, 5020 Salzburg.

Bodenhöfer, Univ.-Prof. Dr. Hans-Joachim,
   Universität Klagenfurt, Universitätstrasse 67, 9010 Klagenfurt.

Clement, Univ.-Prof. Dr. Werner,
   University of Economics, Franz-Klein-Gasse 1, 1190 Vienna.

Embling, Prof. John F.,
   The Old Rectory, Wixoe, Bathorn End, Halstead, Essex 009 4-AU Great Britain.

Fletzberger, Min.-Rat. Dr. Stefan,
   Federal Ministry of Social Affairs, Stubenring 1, 1010 Vienna.

Fuchshuber, Dkfm. Dr. Gerhard,
   Member of the Working Party on Education Policy of the Association of Austrian Industrialists, Schwarzenberg-Platz 4, 1030 Vienna.

Giller, Mag. Joachim,
   Secretary of the FPÖ Group in the National Council, Parlament, 1017 Vienna.

Heitger, Univ.-Prof. Dr. Marian,
   Institute for Pedagogics at Vienna University, Garnisongasse 3/8, 1090 Vienna.

Hofinger, Gustav,
   Deputy Director, Chamber of Wage and Salary Earners in Upper Austria, Volksgartenstrasse 40, 4020 Linz.

Höllinger, Dr. Sigurd,
   Federal Ministry of Science and Research, Head of the Planning and Statistics Department, Minoritenplatz 5, 1010 Vienna.

Jedina-Palombini, Prof. Dr. Auguste,
   Head of the Education Policy Department of the Association of Austrian Industrialists, Schwarzenbergplatz 4, 1030 Vienna.

Jochum, Dr. Manfred,
    Adult Education Department of the Federal Ministry of Education
    and Art, Wallnerstrasse 8, 1010 Vienna.

John, Min.-Rat. Dipl.-Ing. Werner,
    Head of Department II/9 of the Federal Ministry of Education
    and Art, Minoritenplatz 5, 1010 Vienna.

Kempf, Dr. Erwin, OECD, Château de la Muette, 2, rue André Pascal,
    Paris 75016, France.

Kellermann, Univ.-Prof. Dr. Paul,
    Universität Klagenfurt, Universitätsstrasse 67, 9010 Klagenfurt.

Kienast, Günther,
    Institute for Education and Economics, Uraniastrasse 4, 1010 Vienna.

Klar, Dr. Rudolf,
    Institute for Economic Development, Hoher Markt 3, 1010 Vienna.

Klement, Dr. Karl,
    Training College for Primary Teachers Baden, Mathias-Corvinus-
    Gasse 11 a, 3100 St. Pölten.

Knittler-Lux, Dr. Ursula,
    Association of Austrian People's Universities, Rudolfsplatz 8,
    1010 Vienna.

Königshofer, Dr. Nikolaus,
    Director of the Federal Institute for Adult Education St. Wolfgang,
    5350 Strobl.

Kowalski, Dr. Peter,
    Institute for promoting Employment, Wipplingerstrasse 35,
    1010 Vienna.

Leitner, Sekt. Chef Mag. Leo,
    Head of Section I of the Federal Ministry of Education and Art,
    Minoritenplatz 5, 1010 Vienna.

Lenz, Dr. Werner,
    Institute for Pedagogics at Vienna University, Garnisongasse 3/8,
    1090 Vienna.

Lowak, Min.-OKoär Heinz,
    Adult Education Department of the Federal Ministry of Education
    and Art, Wallnerstrasse 8, 1010 Vienna.

Mezriczky, Dr. Gerald,
    Secretary of the Austrian Agricultural Workers' Assembly,
    Dominikanerbastei 21, 1010 Vienna.

Mühlhauser, Hans,
    Head of the ÖGB Educational Institute Neuwaldegg,
    Neuwaldeggerstrasse, 1170 Vienna.

Noszek, Dr. Friedrich,
   Institute for Rural Further Education, Löwelstrasse 12, 1010 Vienna.

Partisch, Min.-Rat. Dipl.-Ing. Dr. Franz,
   Head of Department I/12 of the Federal Ministry of Education and
   Art, Minoritenplatz 5, 1010 Vienna.

Pieper, Helmut, SPÖ, Dr.-Karl-Renner-Institut, Rechtes Salzachufer 30,
   5020 Salzburg.

Piskaty, Dr. Georg,
   Science and Education Policy Department of the Federal Chamber
   of Commerce, Opernring 1/E/7, 1010 Vienna.

Prandstetter, Dr. Edmund, Hochstrasse 27, 1238 Vienna.

Rehn, Dr. Gösta, SOFI-Fack, 10405 Stockholm, Sweden.

Schiffkorn, wHR. Prof. Dr. Aldemar,
   Head of the Development Centre of the Upper Austria Adult
   Education Association, Landstrasse 31, 4020 Linz.

Schneider, Direktor Dr. Gerold,
   Federal Trade Academy and Federal Trade School, Linz, 4020 Linz.

Schuller, Tom, OECD, Château de la Muette, 2, rue André Pascal,
   Paris 75016, France.

Sengenberger, Dr. Werner,
   Institute for Social Science Research, Jakob-Klarstrasse 9,
   Munich 13, Fed. Rep. of Germany.

Steinbacher, Mag. Walter,
   Planning and Statistics Department of the Federal Ministry of
   Science and Research, Minoritenplatz 5, 1010 Vienna.

Steuer, Sekt.-Rat. Mag. Heinz,
   Department 53 of the Federal Ministry of Education and Art,
   Wallnerstrasse 8, 1010 Vienna.

Vanas, Mag. Norbert,
   ÖVP-Klub, Parlament, 1010 Vienna.

Wenisch, Prof. Dr. Ernst,
   Head of the Development Centre of the Salzburg Adult Education
   Association, Rudolfskai 48/II, 5020 Salzburg.

Wicher, Mag. Anita,
   Society for Economic Studies, Association for promoting Education,
   Bauernmarkt 21/13, 1010 Vienna.

OECD SALES AGENTS
DÉPOSITAIRES DES PUBLICATIONS DE L'OCDE

ARGENTINA – ARGENTINE
Carlos Hirsch S.R.L., Florida 165,
BUENOS-AIRES. ☎ 33-1787-2391 Y 30-7122

AUSTRALIA – AUSTRALIE
International B.C.N. Library Suppliers Pty Ltd.,
161 Sturt St., South MELBOURNE, Vic. 3205. ☎ 699-6388
658 Pittwater Road, BROOKVALE NSW 2100. ☎ 938 2267

AUSTRIA – AUTRICHE
Gerold and Co., Graben 31, WIEN I. ☎ 52.22.35

BELGIUM – BELGIQUE
Librairie des Sciences,
Coudenberg 76-78, B 1000 BRUXELLES 1. ☎ 512-05-60

BRAZIL – BRÉSIL
Mestre Jou S.A., Rua Guaipá 518,
Caixa Postal 24090, 05089 SAO PAULO 10. ☎ 261-1920
Rua Senador Dantas 19 s/205-6, RIO DE JANEIRO GB.
☎ 232-07. 32

CANADA
Renouf Publishing Company Limited,
2182 St. Catherine Street West,
MONTREAL, Quebec H3H 1M7 ☎ (514) 937-3519

DENMARK – DANEMARK
Munksgaards Boghandel,
Nørregade 6, 1165 KØBENHAVN K. ☎ (01) 12 69 70

FINLAND – FINLANDE
Akateeminen Kirjakauppa
Keskuskatu 1, 00100 HELSINKI 10. ☎ 625.901

FRANCE
Bureau des Publications de l'OCDE,
2 rue André-Pascal, 75775 PARIS CEDEX 16.
☎ 524.81.67
Principal correspondant :
13602 AIX-EN-PROVENCE : Librairie de l'Université.
☎ 26.18.08

GERMANY – ALLEMAGNE
Verlag Weltarchiv G.m.b.H.
D 2000 HAMBURG 36, Neuer Jungfernstieg 21.
☎ 040-35-62-500

GREECE – GRÈCE
Librairie Kauffmann, 28 rue du Stade,
ATHÈNES 132. ☎ 322.21.60

HONG-KONG
Government Information Services,
Sales and Publications Office, Beaconsfield House, 1st floor,
Queen's Road, Central. ☎ H-233191

ICELAND – ISLANDE
Snaebjörn Jónsson and Co., h.f.,
Hafnarstraeti 4 and 9, P.O.B. 1131, REYKJAVIC.
☎ 13133/14281/11936

INDIA – INDE
Oxford Book and Stationery Co.:
NEW DELHI, Scindia House. ☎ 45896
CALCUTTA, 17 Park Street. ☎ 240832

IRELAND - IRLANDE
Eason and Son, 40 Lower O'Connell Street,
P.O.B. 42. DUBLIN 1. ☎ 74 39 35

ISRAËL
Emanuel Brown: 35 Allenby Road, TEL AVIV. ☎ 51049/54082
also at:
9. Shlomzion Hamalka Street, JERUSALEM. ☎ 234807
48 Nahlath Benjamin Street, TEL AVIV. ☎ 53276

ITALY – ITALIE
Libreria Commissionaria Sansoni:
Via Lamarmora 45, 50121 FIRENZE. ☎ 579751
Via Bartolini 29, 20155 MILANO. ☎ 365083
Sous-dépositaires :
Editrice e Libreria Herder,
Piazza Montecitorio 120, 00 186 ROMA. ☎ 674628
Libreria Hoepli, Via Hoepli 5, 20121 MILANO. ☎ 365446
Libreria Lattes, Via Garibaldi 3, 10122 TORINO. ☎ 519274
La diffusione delle edizioni OCDE è inoltre assicurata dalle migliori librerie nelle città più importanti.

JAPAN – JAPON
OECD Publications Centre,
Akasaka Park Building, 2-3-4 Akasaka, Minato-ku,
TOKYO 107. ☎ 586-2016

KOREA - CORÉE
Pan Korea Book Corporation,
P.O.Box n°101 Kwangwhamun, SÉOUL. ☎ 72-7369

LEBANON – LIBAN
Documenta Scientifica/Redico,
Edison Building, Bliss Street, P.O.Box 5641, BEIRUT.
☎ 354429 – 344425

THE NETHERLANDS – PAYS-BAS
W.P. Van Stockum,
Buitenhof 36, DEN HAAG. ☎ 070-65.68.08

NEW ZEALAND - NOUVELLE-ZÉLANDE
The Publications Manager,
Government Printing Office,
WELLINGTON: Mulgrave Street (Private Bag),
World Trade Centre, Cubacade, Cuba Street,
Rutherford House, Lambton Quay. ☎ 737-320
AUCKLAND: Rutland Street (P.O.Box 5344), ☎ 32.919
CHRISTCHURCH: 130 Oxford Tce (Private Bag). ☎ 50.331
HAMILTON: Barton Street (P.O.Box 857), ☎ 80.103
DUNEDIN: T & G Building, Princes Street (P.O.Box 1104).
☎ 78.294

NORWAY – NORVÈGE
Johan Grundt Tanums Bokhandel,
Karl Johansgate 41/43, OSLO 1. ☎ 02-332980

PAKISTAN
Mirza Book Agency, 65 Shahrah Quaid-E-Azam, LAHORE 3.
☎ 66839

PHILIPPINES
R.M. Garcia Publishing House, 903 Quezon Blvd. Ext.,
QUEZON CITY, P.O.Box 1860 – MANILA. ☎ 99.98.47

PORTUGAL
Livraria Portugal, Rua do Carmo 70-74, LISBOA 2. ☎ 360582/3

SPAIN – ESPAGNE
Mundi-Prensa Libros, S.A.
Castelló 37, Apartado 1223, MADRID-1. ☎ 275.46.55
Libreria Bastinos, Pelayo, 52, BARCELONA 1. ☎ 222.06.00

SWEDEN – SUÈDE
AB CE FRITZES KUNGL HOVBOKHANDEL,
Box 16 356, S 103 27 STH, Regeringsgatan 12,
DS STOCKHOLM. ☎ 08/23 89 00

SWITZERLAND – SUISSE
Librairie Payot, 6 rue Grenus, 1211 GENÈVE 11. ☎ 022-31.89.50

TAIWAN – FORMOSE
National Book Company,
84-5 Sing Sung Rd., Sec. 3, TAIPEI 107. ☎ 321.0698

TURKEY – TURQUIE
Librairie Hachette,
469 Istiklal Caddesi, Beyoglu, ISTANBUL. ☎ 44.94.70
et 14 E Ziya Gökalp Caddesi, ANKARA. ☎ 12.10.80

UNITED KINGDOM – ROYAUME-UNI
H.M. Stationery Office, P.O.B. 569,
LONDON SEI 9 NH. ☎ 01-928-6977, Ext.410
or
49 High Holborn, LONDON WC1V 6 HB (personal callers)
Branches at: EDINBURGH, BIRMINGHAM, BRISTOL,
MANCHESTER, CARDIFF, BELFAST.

UNITED STATES OF AMERICA
OECD Publications Center, Suite 1207, 1750 Pennsylvania Ave.,
N.W. WASHINGTON, D.C.20006. ☎ (202)298-8755

VENEZUELA
Libreria del Este, Avda. F. Miranda 52, Edificio Galipán,
CARACAS 106. ☎ 32 23 01/33 26 04/33 24 73

YUGOSLAVIA – YOUGOSLAVIE
Jugoslovenska Knjiga, Terazije 27, P.O.B. 36, BEOGRAD.
☎ 621-992

Les commandes provenant de pays où l'OCDE n'a pas encore désigné de dépositaire peuvent être adressées à :
OCDE, Bureau des Publications, 2 rue André-Pascal, 75775 PARIS CEDEX 16.
Orders and inquiries from countries where sales agents have not yet been appointed may be sent to:
OECD, Publications Office, 2 rue André-Pascal, 75775 PARIS CEDEX 16.

OECD PUBLICATIONS
2, rue André-Pascal, 75775 Paris Cedex 16

No. 39.377 1977

PRINTED IN FRANCE